Does Everything Happen for a Reason, God?

Lilly Horigan

Lilly Books
Bolivar, Ohio

Published by Lilly Books, LLC, PO Box 223, Bolivar, OH 44612

ISBN: 978-1-64683-004-6

Contents

Introduction

Book Outline

1: Why Suffering is a Part of this World

2: Free Will

3: God's Sovereignty

4: The Inevitability of Suffering

5: When Suffering is Unexpected

6: Navigating Troubled Waters

7: Benefits of Suffering

8: Suffering as a Friend

9: Suffering Increases Strength

10: Suffering Gets Our Attention

11: Profiting from Suffering

12: Suffering Brings Clarity

13: Conclusion

14: Next Steps

References

Connect

About The Author

Books By This Author

Introduction

If you are going through something right now that has you in a mental or spiritual mess, go ahead and skip this introduction for now. I totally understand. However, please note that all the information in this booklet is from my own research at home, along with a cup of coffee, my Bible, and favorite books from my favorite Bible teachers. I am not a theologian (maybe an amateur or want-to-be one). Blessings to you as you aim to understand if everything happens for a reason.

WHY I AM WRITING THIS BOOK

This booklet was born out of confusion as I sat in my local church listening to one of my favorite pastors tell his congregation that everything *does not* happen for a reason. It rocked my world, and I sat stunned. The statement pierced the bubble within me that believed that God was always in control of everything. Was I wrong? Was the pastor? Did I misunderstand sovereignty? I had to figure it out.

Just a couple of years after coming to Christ at the age of 24, I visited a church whose pastor said that anyone could take communion, including those who had not yet accepted

Christ as their Savior. He stated that Christ had died for all and so all could participate. I didn't know much about communion, as I was just a babe in Christ, and was not yet a member of a solid, Biblically-based church. And who was I to question this pastor who had decades more knowledge on God than I did?

Soon after that, we had a death in our family. Our lost loved one was Catholic and her funeral followed all of the traditional Catholic practices, including communion. When it came time for me to go forward, I leaned toward my anti-Christ mother, who claimed to be a cultural Catholic, and asked her if she was going to go forward. She said no, and I informed her that communion was for all. She knew in her heart, however, that it was not for her. She did not want to consume the symbolic body or blood of Christ. She did not follow Him.

With time, and a home church founded on sound Biblical doctrine, I learned the truth. Communion was for believers. From that point forward, I researched everything I heard that gave me any inkling that something was wrong or off. I was angry with myself for just taking what that man had said as gospel—he was human and prone to error, too.

My next opportunity to research a questionable comment in my local church came when I was told that women could not lead the Bible studies at Sunday School. I studied, read, and found every Scripture in God's Word about teaching and women. Bottom line: Jesus changed the world for women and taught that we are equal with men, not physically, but with varying abilities that can indeed include teaching and telling. My husband would be the first to tell anyone that I have a gift for leading, teaching, and facilitating groups. He prefers to only lead if absolutely necessary. He is a reluctant leader, but a good one none the less. So, he defers to me when we lead small groups because he understands our gifts are different. If you believe women can't lead and train groups, churches, and men; research and pray for confirmation and/or revelation.

Since that time, I've had many opportunities to research random, unbiblical comments by friends (like one friend who told me it was idolatry to pray to Jesus) and questionable teachings from the pulpit (like one pastor who said it is impossible to please God) in hopes of confirming or correcting what was said in my own heart and home.

Do I take what I have learned to those people? Rarely, and it depends on our relationship. I mostly pray for them and ask God to bring correction into their hearts via people they admire and trust. I also aim to not slander those people, complain, or stir up any tension within my church per God's direction. In the end, I hope that my attention to detail, magnification of the teachings of seasoned believers in Christ, and obsession for research can help many people see what God says about the topics.

I don't have a degree in theology. Although I attended a Christian college, I majored in leadership and management. Everything I have learned has been through God's work in me over the past 20 years. Therefore, I am not claiming perfection or rightness in every topic. My hope is that others would look to the Word of God, trusted Biblical scholars, and pray for revelation to determine if what they are hearing is the truth.

I believe that if we have a willing heart to learn what is true and honoring, God will bless that with knowledge and wisdom. It is only from Him that we receive them anyway.

The authors and books I reference in the following pages are those that have shown, through their messages and works, that they have a heart to know God's Word and share it to the best of their ability. This book is not written to help convince people that God exists. (Can I save you some time? He does!) The purpose of this book is to tackle one question from a Christian perspective: Does Everything Happen for a Reason?

A MINI TESTIMONY

I was raised in a very peculiar family. I had a positive, encouraging "self-made" father who loved me, supported me, and did his best to raise me with the values he felt were the most important in life: get a good eduction (he was a teacher who had taught himself to read), don't suffer (he studied Buddhism for years), and do not lie, cheat, steal, or commit adultery (he was an Irish-Catholic). I never heard the rest of the Ten Commandments. Although he was Catholic, we were just Easter/Christmas attendees. There was no Jesus in our home and no actual talk of God that I can remember.

My mother and step-father were secular humanists first and foremost. My step-father was also an astrologer, and he taught me why so many things were wrong with me via my chart and sign. They did not believe there was a God unless He was possibly in the trees and every little thing, as my mom would say during her Pantheism streaks. They believed Jesus was just a man, and that almost everything could be explained by the stars.

To say the least, I was a very confused teenager, but I gravitated more toward secular humanism as I got older. I mocked Christians and faiths that believed there was a God at all and lived like I was the god of my life.

Thankfully, God created my personality and also its love of learning. It was while I was in the Navy that I began to really love learning new things. I took guitar lessons. I went to college at night. I began quilting. I learned about Wicca. I attended meetings with Jehovah's Witnesses. I began talking to friends who had actual relationships with God and believed in Jesus. I changed from persecuting Christians to asking them questions.

I believe God put that learning and seeking heart into me! At twenty-four, after a couple of years of talking to dear friends, attending a Methodist church with my boyfriend, and knowing I was missing something/someone in my life, I accepted Christ.

I was on fire for Jesus that year and it has continued ever since. I am now 43 as I write this book, and I am addicted to reading, studying, and learning. I try, of course, to apply what I have learned. Some days that is easier said than done. I would love to tell you I had a huge impact on my family for Jesus, but I believe that I am still the only Christian. I pray that someday I will have been the first, but not the only.

When God gave me my choleric-melancholic and questioning personality, He also allowed a pre-disposition to anxiety and perfectionism. My environment added insecurity, fear of failure, and control issues. I aim to use all of these for the benefit of the Kingdom of God. This book is the product of the questioner, perfectionist, and control-freak within me hoping to help other Christians understand a common saying we hear in our everyday lives either in the positive (everything happens for a reason), or in the negative (it's all luck).

I believe our weaknesses, whether born with them or learned over time, and our suffering have (spoiler alert) happened for a reason and can be strengths. Taking time to figure out how you can use those weaknesses for God and others is worth all the effort you can put into it. However, the best way to begin is to be able to know in your own heart if those things truly have a purpose.

BOOK FORMAT

This book is setup with smaller chapters with reflection questions to allow for use in a daily God time or study group. To get the most out of the book, do not skip over the reflection prompts. Answer each question. That is where the growth will happen in your relationship and confidence in Christ as it pertains to suffering.

I purposely chose the Amplified version of the Bible for this book. I understand many are not familiar with this version; however, I have found it to be very useful to see Scripture in a different way.

Book Outline

1. Why Suffering is a Part of this World
2. Free Will
3. God's Sovereignty
4. The Inevitability of Suffering
    A. Why We Suffer (Beyond the Fall)
    B. Duration
5. When Suffering is Unexpected
6. Navigating Troubled Waters
7. Benefits of Suffering
    A. Learning to Trust
    B. Growing in Wisdom
    C. Less Anxiety
    D. Increased Gratitude
    E. Inner Calm
    F. Greater Courage
8. Suffering as a Friend
9. Suffering Increases Strength
10. Suffering Gets Our Attention
11. Profiting from Suffering
12. Suffering Brings Clarity
13. Conclusion
14. Next Steps

~ Chapter 1 ~

Why Suffering is a Part of this World

I hate to start the first chapter with such a bummer title, but the inevitability of suffering is part of everyone's life. Therefore, I believe it is highly beneficial to understand the details of suffering. If you feel you have not suffered at all in your life up to this point, then praise God. Eventually, however, you will lose a loved one, deal with a sickness in your own life, or endure the numerous other types of suffering that exist in this world. We can suffer with the consequences of our own choices and failures. We may suffer from the betrayal of a loved one, the anger of a bully, or the violence of a stranger. We may suffer for our faith.

The ways we can suffer are innumerable. The good news is that we can learn to live in peace and joy despite the hardships that come our way. The common question I think most atheists ask Christians is why bad things happen to good people. Knowing how to answer this question can be the first glimpse a non-believer sees of the joy and hope that is found in Christ.

When the question is asked by a seeker, it can lead to a

great discussion. When it is asked by one who is anti-Christ, it can lead to persecution (for most people, it is verbal). Christians who face persecution (suffering) for their faith need to face it with patience, endurance, and steadfastness. Understanding that each encounter has a purpose and a reason can grow and develop these attributes.

But if [one is ill-treated and suffers] as a Christian [which he is contemptuously called], let him not be ashamed, but give glory to God that he is [deemed worthy to suffer] in His name (1 Peter 4:16).

Learning to live with peace and joy despite hardship is a worthy pursuit, and it does not come naturally. Since everyone will suffer in some way, our knowledge in this area can be the tool God uses, not only in our own lives but also in the lives of those within our circle of influence. Christians need to understand the sovereignty of God and why they can trust His purpose in everything.

Remember [earnestly] also your Creator [that you are not your own, but His property now] in the days of your youth, before the evil days come or the years draw near when you will say [of physical pleasures], I have no enjoyment in them (Ecclesiastes 12:1).

Although this book is primarily for Christians, it can be a

great resource for any seekers who want to understand what God says about life and Christ in the midst of tragedies. Everyone lives in a fallen world, and it is not the world God gave us originally. If you don't know the story of the fall, go ahead and read chapters two and three of the book of Genesis.

But of the tree of the knowledge of good and evil and blessing and calamity you shall not eat, for in the day that you eat of it you shall surely die (Genesis 2:17).

Because of man's rebellion against God's Word in the garden, all the world suffers. Everyone has alienation from God, self-deception, broken relationships, and exhausting physical labor. God is holy and He judged sin just as He warned Adam He would. Ken Ham of Answers in Genesis (AIG) stated, "In doing so [judging sin], God has given us a taste of life without Him—a world that is running down—a world full of death and suffering. Man, in essence, forfeited his right to live."

When someone asks you why there is evil in the world, the answer is because of this fall and sin. And because there is evil in the world, there is also physical and emotional pain, too. Since everyone's life (including Eve's) came through Adam and from God, it is God Who owns us and gives us our very being—we should follow Him and not our own ways. Adam and Eve had the perfect parent and the perfect environment, so they could not blame their upbringing for their failure. Eve made a decision to disobey. Adam made the decision to follow his wife into disobedience. I am very confident that I also would have made the wrong choice in that perfect environment.

We are all part of Adam's family, and so we all have sin within us. Sin is passed from generation to generation through blood—not flesh. Our blood was only produced within us once the sperm from our human, sinful father was introduced to our mother's egg—creating life. Therefore, each baby has a separate blood line from his/her mother.

The beauty of how a baby has a separate blood line from the mother leads us to the importance of Jesus' conception and birth. Jesus was born just as we were born; he grew as we grew. But it was how Jesus needed to be conceived that required God's intervention. God knew what His Son required on earth and how our bodies worked. So, God begot His only Son here on earth so that Jesus would not have a human father and his blood would not be tainted with sin.

When we suffer, therefore, it is because of the sin in the heart (literally, the blood) of every person. Sin is the root cause. We all inherited it and cannot get away or purge it from within us. This is why we don't have to teach our children how to lie, complain, etc. There may be many additional reasons why we suffer, which this book will discuss, but ultimately there is suffering in the world because there is sin in the world.

Chuck Swindoll, in his book *Embraced by the Spirit,* created a list of "The 5 Suffering Laws Regarding Sickness, Health, and Healing" which begins with original sin due to the fall.

The 5 Suffering Laws Regarding Sickness, Health, and Healing by Chuck Swindoll

Law 1) There are two classifications of sin: original and personal.

Law 2) Original sin introduced suffering, illness, and death to the human race.

Law 3) Sometimes there is a direct relationship between personal sins and sickness.

Law 4) Sometimes there is no relationship between personal sin and sickness.

Law 5) It is not God's will that everyone be healed.

Corollary to Law 5: Sometimes it is God's will that someone is healed.

Has there been anyone who has suffered without any cause?

Yes. Jesus.

For our sake He made Christ [virtually] to be sin Who knew no sin, so that in and through Him we might become [endued with, viewed as being in, and examples of] the righteousness of God [what we ought to be, approved and acceptable and in right relationship with Him, by His Goodness] (2 Corinthians 5:21).

Jesus is the only case of a person suffering for no reason. He was completely innocent, and He willingly suffered so He could reconcile us to God. Billy Graham wrote, "Jesus has defeated the three enemies of man—sin, Satan, and death. While they are still present in this life, Christ has conquered them all" (*Where I Am*).

Is everyone now reconciled to God because of Christ? No, but it is available to all. Everyone is not automatically reconciled because, in addition to giving us our life and His Son, God also gave us all free will.

Chapter 1: Reflection Prompts

1. Go back and read through the first chapter.
   (a) Write the points of interest.

   _____

   _____

   _____

   (b) Note the Scripture references.

   _____

   _____

   _____

   (c) List any questions you have on the topic of why suffering exists that the text did not answer or is leading you to research further.

   _____

   _____

   _____

2. Do you struggle in your relationship with God when good people suffer?

_____

_____

_____

3. Read Romans 3:10. Who does God list as being good (righteous, just) in this world?

_____

4. Have you ever met anyone who believes God exists but does not think he/she has any sin? What does God say of people who believe they have no sin? See 1 John 1:8.

_____

_____

_____

5. Look up and define the word sovereignty.

_____

_____

_____

6. Research how a baby's blood is separate from his/her mother's blood. Does this help explain how Jesus is both fully man and fully God?

_____

_____

_____

7. Re-read the five suffering laws by Swindoll. Is there one you struggle with when you read it? Why?

_____

_____

_____

~ Chapter 2 ~

Free Will

God didn't create robots on this earth—humans that must love and serve Him without choice—even though He had all the right to make them in such a way. He chose to create people with free will.

...I have set before you life and death, the blessings and the curse; therefore choose life, that you and your descendants may live (Deuteronomy 30:19).

Like any good father, God knew we would need guidance to do the right thing: to choose life (i.e., Christ).

Jesus said, I am the Way and the Truth and the Life; no one comes to the Father except by (through) Me (John 14:6).

God knew our hearts and our fallen bent toward our own way, our inner pride, and our stubbornness. Choosing to believe would have its benefits and He didn't want us to miss that, so He gave a very obvious hint of what we should choose: life. The biggest benefit of choosing life is, of course, eternity with Him.

For God so greatly loved and dearly prized the world that He [even] gave up His only begotten (unique) Son, so that whoever believes in (trusts in, clings to, relies on) Him shall not perish (come to destruction, be lost) but have eternal (everlasting) life (John 3:16).

Besides eternity, God gives us the Holy Spirit. He is our Helper and the One Who guides us as we develop His amazing fruit (love, joy, peace, patience, kindness, goodness, faithfulness, gentleness, and self control as mentioned in Ephesians). Believers in Christ also have the opportunity of knowing God's good and perfect will, trusting in His love for them, receiving His blessings, and so much more.

I appeal to you therefore, brethren, and beg of you in view of [all] the mercies of God, to make a decisive dedication of your bodies [presenting all your members and faculties] as a living sacrifice, holy (devoted, consecrated) and well pleasing to God, which is your reasonable (rational, intelligent) service and spiritual worship. Do not be conformed to this world (this age), [fashioned after and adapted to its external, superficial customs], but be transformed (changed) by the [entire] renewal of your mind [by its new ideals and is new attitude], so that you may prove [for yourselves] what is the good and acceptable and perfect will of God, even the thing which is good and acceptable and perfect [in His sight for you] (Romans 12:1-2).

Choosing life by putting faith in Jesus Christ means joy, protection, and blessing. God is the believer's shield. He gives gladness, peace, safety, forgiveness, compassion, and blessings. However, He did not promise a life without trouble; quite the opposite.

I have told you these things, so that in Me you may have [perfect] peace and confidence. In the world you have tribulations and trials and distress and frustration; but be of good cheer [take courage; be confident, certain, undaunted]! For I have overcome the world, [I have deprived it of power to harm you and have conquered it for you] (John 16:33).

Are you wondering how God can give protection and safety while also allowing trouble? Realistically, we have no idea how much God is protecting us from in any given day. Promising protection does not mean a life without trouble. He knows what He is protecting you from and what trouble He allows to touch you.

But let all those who take refuge and put their trust in You rejoice; let them ever sing and shout for joy, because You make a covering over them and defend them; let those also who love Your name be joyful in You and be in high spirits. For You, Lord, will bless the [uncompromisingly] righteous [him who is upright and in right standing with You}; as with a shield You will surround him with goodwill (pleasure and favor) (Psalm 5:11-12).

So, what about the person who has decided to reject Christ as Lord and Savior? They are using their right to reject Him and choose death. Choosing death means choosing to stay separated from God for eternity. Every person will spend eternity somewhere and rejecting God not only means separation, but also defeat, isolation, and instability.

Therefore the wicked [those disobedient and living without God] shall not stand [justified] in the judgment, nor sinners in the congregation of the righteous [those who are upright and in right standing with God]. For the Lord knows and is fully acquainted with the way of the righteous, but the way of the ungodly [those living outside God's will] shall perish (end in ruin and come to nought) (Psalm 1:5-6).

Can God draw someone, who doesn't want to believe in Him, to Himself? C.S. Lewis describes his coming to Christ as a fight that he longed to escape from but couldn't. This is a description of the Calvinist teaching of irresistible grace.

Remember, God is sovereign and the ability to save whomever He wills would be within His right and ability.

However, this book is only meant to be a stepping stone to understanding if everything happens for a reason. If you are interested in learning more about irresistible grace, please visit the website of one of my mentors, Ray Stedman. His *Foundations of Faith* series is a fantastic resource for understanding the Bible, God, Jesus, man, redemption, the Holy Spirit, the church, Christian responsibility, and the resurrection.

CHAPTER 2: REFLECTION PROMPTS

1. Go back and read through the second chapter.
   (a) Write the points of interest.

   _____

   _____

   _____

   (b) Note the Scripture references.

   _____

   _____

   _____

   (c) List any questions you have on the topic of free will that the text did not answer or is leading you to research further.

   _____

   _____

   _____

2. We are not God's robots, yet He is a sovereign creator. He has made it clear that there is no other way of having a relationship with Him than through belief (faith) and acceptance of Jesus Christ as Lord and Savior. All are lost without Him. Can you think of any similarities between God creating humans with free will, while maintaining His sovereignty, with the relationship between a parent and a child?

_____

_____

_____

3. Research and define the word propitiation. Use a website or concordance app to see where it is used in the Bible. Why is it important?

_____

_____

_____

4. Have you accepted Christ as your Lord and Savior? (If not, go and speak to a known Christian in your life that is aiming to live Christlike, find a local church that believes in sound biblical doctrine, or check out websites from authors quoted in this book.)

_____

_____

_____

5. Paraphrase Romans 12: 1-2. How can you apply it to your life?

_____

_____

_____

6. What does it mean that God *begot* His Son? This word is often ignored when John 3:16 is read or spoken, but it is the

key to understanding why Jesus is fully God and fully man. (For the best understanding of this word and its importance, read C.S. Lewis's book *Mere Christianity*.)

_____

_____

_____

7. Dig Deeper: According to followers of John Calvin, he taught five points. What are they?

_____

_____

_____

8. I personally agree with Ray Stedman that one point is not a teaching of Calvin, but a teaching of his followers and that it is not consistent with God's teachings in His Word. Which one is it? (Search for Ray Stedman's Foundation's of Faith: Regarding Redemption message series for the answer. RayStedman.org)

_____

_____

_____

Note: Although the remainder of this book is written for the Christian reader, it can also help those who have not made the decision to follow Christ. It is my prayer, however, that you don't wait much longer. There is no guarantee you will have the opportunity tomorrow.

God is your protector, He is the one who preserves your life from hour to hour, day to day, year to year. He is in charge of keeping you alive on this earth until the split second that He desires for you to be in eternity with Him. God has a plan to bless you on this earth and reward you in eternity. Everything you experience, even those things that you might label 'bad,' God can and will turn to good if only you will trust Him to be your sovereign Lord (Charles Stanley, Finding Peace).

~ Chapter 3 ~
God's Sovereignty

Charles Stanley wrote, "God is absolutely sovereign—which means that nothing related to you is beyond His watchful eye and loving care." Despite all the loneliness in the world or the pain one may endure, God loves each person He has created. He is not shocked by anything and is in full control of each heartbeat and breath we take. Because He is sovereign, it is from Him that wisdom, power, woe, and well-being proceed.

To the one and only God, our Savior through Jesus Christ our Lord, be glory (splendor), majesty, might and dominion, and power and authority, before all time and now and forever (unto all the ages of eternity). Amen (so be it) (Jude 1:25).

For with God nothing is ever impossible and no word from God shall be without power or impossible of fulfillment (Luke 1:37).

It can be frustrating for Christians to see the "smart" people of the world not credit God for their discoveries, intelligence, or knowledge. After all, God allowed all of it. Instead, they credit their hard work—which may or may not have been a part— to luck, karma, or the universe. However, this is not limited to non-believers. How many Christians do the same when they say how lucky they are? Therefore, God often uses the "simple" of this world to show His power.

But to those who are called, whether Jew or Greek (Gentile), Christ [is] the Power of God and the Wisdom of God. [This is] because the foolish thing [that has its source in] God is wiser than men, and the weak thing [that springs] from God is stronger than men (1 Corinthians 1:24-25).

Eventually, in His own way, God will get the glory.

[God] disarmed the principalities and powers that were ranged against us and made a bold display and public example of them, triumphing over them in Him and in it [the cross] (Colossians 2:15).

I prefer most of this book to be God's Word and the words of wiser men and women in the faith that I have learned so much from over the years; hence the subtitle of the book, as I feel completely inadequate to write about God's sovereignty. This is not only because I have limited knowledge and time studying the subject, but I often struggle to live by what God so plainly states. With my anxiety disorder and personality type, it is difficult for me to apply the truth in circumstances as they happen. So, this research and the daily habit of writing this book are ways I can preach His Word back to myself. It is easy to forget what we, as believers, need to remember.

Is it not out of the mouth of the Most High that evil and good both proceed [adversity and prosperity, physical evil or misfortune and physical good or happiness]? (Lamentations 3:38)

Consider it wholly joyful, my brethren, whenever you are enveloped in or encounter trials of any sort or fall into various temptations. Be assured and understand that the trial and proving of your faith bring out endurance and steadfastness and patience (James 1:2-3).

If our world is turned inside out or shaken, it is God who has allowed it. He may have allowed it for one reason or a dozen. Only He knows, and, if He wills it, He may show us a small glimpse of "the why" while we are here on earth. Whatever the reason(s); however, He always cares and He comforts us through it all.

Blessed be the God and Father of our Lord Jesus Christ, the Father of sympathy (pity and mercy) and the God [Who is the Source] of every comfort (consolation and encouragement). Who comforts (consoles and encourages) us in every trouble (calamity and affliction), so that we may also be able to comfort (console and encourage) those who are in any kind of trouble or distress... (2 Corinthians 1:3-4a)

Amazingly, the God of the universe purposely works through the people He created. Billy Graham wrote, "It is staggering to think that God has entrusted to people like us--redeemed sinners--the responsibility of carrying out His divine purpose" (*Where I Am*).

David, a man after God's own heart who made many, many mistakes and suffered the consequences of them, understood that everything belonged to God including the finest moments.

Therefore David blessed the Lord before all the assembly and said, Be praised, adored, and thanked, O Lord, the God of Israel our [forefather], forever and ever. Yours, O Lord, is the greatness and the power and the glory and the victory and the majesty, for all that is in the heavens and the earth is Yours; Yours is the kingdom, O Lord, and Yours it is to be exalted as Head over all. Both riches and honor come from You, and You reign over all. In Your hands are power and might; in Your hands it is to make great and to give strength to all

(1 Chronicles 29:10-12).

Whatever we are going through, believers in Christ can trust that God goes before them. We are His family and a good father doesn't leave His children.

Fear not [there is nothing to fear], for I am with you; do not look around you in terror and be dismayed, for I am your God. I will strengthen and harden you to difficulties, yes, I will help you; yes, I will hold you up and retain you with My [victorious] right hand of rightness and justice (Isaiah 41:10).

CHAPTER 3: REFLECTION PROMPTS

1. Go back and read through the third chapter.
   (a) Write the points of interest.

   _____

   _____

   _____

   (b) Note the Scripture references.

   _____

   _____

   _____

   (c) List any questions you have on the topic of sovereignty that the text did not answer or is leading you to research further.

   _____

   _____

   _____

2. Do you believe there is anything about you that God does not know or care about?

_____

_____

_____

3. Is it hard for you to fathom that God loves you in all moments (yesterday and tomorrow) as much as He loves you right now? That He loves you just as much as He loves

everyone else?

_____

_____

_____

4. Is there something you are doing to try and earn more of God's love?

_____

_____

_____

5. Do you believe gifts and talents are learned, given, or both? Go on YouTube and research the Polgar sisters. What did their father believe? Adding your faith into the equation, do the results of his theory encourage you? Frustrate you?

_____

_____

_____

6. Do you know someone who is smart or successful and would scoff at believing God had any part of it?

_____

_____

_____

7. Recall a time when you suffered. Looking back, do you see a possible purpose for the suffering? Has anyone,

including yourself, positively benefited from it?

_____

_____

_____

8. Knowing that God goes before you, is there something you have been dreading to do that you should now move forward with?

_____

_____

_____

~ Chapter 4 ~
The Inevitability of Suffering

But though He causes grief, yet will He be moved to compassion according to the multitude of His loving-kindness and tender mercy. For He does not willingly and from His heart afflict or grieve the children of men (Lamentations 3:32-33).

Charles Stanley wrote, "Not only does Jesus provide eternal life when we accept Him as our Savior, He also came to provide us an abundant life. An abundant life is a life filled to overflowing with every good blessing so we can accomplish all the Lord has called us to do and to be in our life."

How do we reconcile these comments? God causes grief, but He shows compassion. He does not afflict willingly, He does not grieve the children of men, and He sent His Son to provide an abundant life. Thankfully, there is no contradiction in God or His Word.

In Romans 8, Paul states that even in our difficulties God's love is real, active, and cannot be severed. Paul knew we would have suffering, and he did not want us to let it impede our faith.

Who shall ever separate us from Christ's love? Shall suffering and affliction and tribulation? Or calamity and distress? Or persecution or hunger or destitution or peril or sword? (Romans 8:35)

David Jeremiah, in his book *God Loves You*, encourages believers in the inevitability of suffering:

Those who trust in the ways and purposes of God will be strengthened in the present and prepared to face whatever the future holds. Suffering is inevitable; it comes to everyone. But only those who live in the certainty that God's love will never let them go are able to accept with confidence and assurance both the troubles of the present and the troubles that may come tomorrow.

Yet amid all these things we are more than conquerors and gain a surpassing victory through Him Who loved us (Romans 8:37).

WHY WE SUFFER (BEYOND THE FALL)

Chuck Swindoll states there are at least three reasons he has found in Paul's words for why we suffer:
1) To be prepared to comfort others
2) To not trust in ourselves
3) To learn to give thanks in everything

Many wonder why bad things happen to good people. But…

There is no one [essentially and perfectly morally] good —except God alone (Mark 10:17b).

What if people, especially Christians, think of others in different terms? Not as good and bad, but as justified and unjustified (those who who have justification available to them, if they choose to accept it). The just and the unjust.

Those who have accepted Christ as Lord are now righteous (made right/justified) in God's eyes. Since all have sinned and are falling short of the honor and glory which God bestows and receives. [All] are justified and made upright and in right standing with God, freely and gratuitously by His grace (His unmerited favor and mercy), through the redemption which is [provided] in Christ Jesus, Whom God put forward [before the eyes of all] as a mercy seat and propitiation by His blood [the cleansing and life-giving sacrifice of atonement and reconciliation to be received] through faith. This was to show God's righteousness because in His divine forbearance He had passed over and ignored former sins without punishment. It was to demonstrate and prove at the present time (in the now season) that He Himself is righteous and that He justifies and accepts as righteous him who has [true] faith in Jesus (Romans

3:23-26).

When we hear someone say and ask, "He/She loved God and believed in Jesus. Why did this happen?," they are unknowingly speaking of the just versus the unjust. Yet, David Jeremiah reminds us of the following truth:

God will send His rain on the just and the unjust, but His children, who recognize and embrace His ways, will know that the rain is cool, refreshing water from heaven. It makes us grow. It gives us joy. And it makes life-real, life-possible in this dry dusty world (Count It All Joy).

Jeremiah is telling Christ-followers that they should see everything—life circumstances, events, etc.—from a different worldview. Christians can learn to reframe the events in this life into an opportunity to trust and have faith in their all-knowing God.

I believe strong faith, steadfast trust, continual reframing, and living with a Christ-mindset takes time, practice, and patience. Someone I respect and admire once told me that I was not making Christ the center of my life since I still struggled with anxiety and worry. I, personally, could not disagree more with that statement. Jesus knew we would struggle, and He told us what to do when that happens:

Come to Me, all you who labor and are heavy-laden and overburdened and I will cause you to rest. [I will ease and relieve and refresh your souls] (Matthew 11:28).

Thankfully, Jesus understands everything we go through and He knows our hearts better than any human walking this earth, including ourselves. He knew we would have trouble.

Though the fig tree may not blossom,
or fruit be on the vines;
Though the labor of the olive may fail,
And the fields yield no food;
Though the flock may be cut off from the fold,
And there be no herd in the stalls—
Yet I will rejoice in the Lord,
I will joy in the God of my salvation
(Habakkuk 3: 17-19).

In other words, for me this verse might say: "God, though my children disobey me; though I have health problems that the doctors don't understand; though my friend has betrayed me; and my brother won't speak to me, I will rejoice in you."

DURATION

We rarely know how long our suffering is going to last, especially with sickness. Therefore, chronically worrying and obsessing about how long it will go on is useless. Having relationship with God and bringing Him your cares and concerns is not useless. He is the only One Who knows the end from the beginning.

Nevertheless, do not let this one fact escape you, beloved, that with the Lord one day is as a thousand years and a thousand years as one day (2 Peter 3:8).

David Jeremiah, in his book *When Your World Falls Apart*, wrote, "[God] will bring resolution in His own time, **according to His own purposes.**"

Charles Stanley, in his book *Finding Peace*, wrote, "Jesus taught His followers that all troubles are passing in nature. Sickness and trouble are for a season and **for a reason.**"

Stanley further explains: "Jesus' very life was for a season and a reason. Even His death and burial in a tomb were only for a season and for a reason. Jesus knew that God permits things to happen in our lives only for a certain period of time and for a particular reason."

CHAPTER 4: REFLECTION PROMPTS

1. Go back and read through the fourth chapter.

(a) Write the points of interest.

_____

_____

_____

(b) Note the Scripture references.

_____

_____

_____

(c) List any questions you have on the topic of the inevitability of suffering that the text did not answer or is leading you to research further.

_____

_____

_____

2. Read Psalm 91. Notice that the rich promises of the Psalm are dependent on meeting the conditions of the first two verses. Read the Psalm again with this in mind. Read verses 9 and 10. After reading of God's sovereignty, do these verses confuse you or reconcile for you that God is ultimately in control?

_____

_____

_____

3. Read 1 Peter 1:6. Our suffering for Christ when we follow God's will is for how long and for what reason?

_____

_____

_____

4. Have you heard of reframing? It is seeing things in a different light. Take a situation right now and reframe it to see the possible good that could come from it. (Consider picking up a book on reframing.)

_____

_____

_____

5. What season are you going through right now? Labeling our situations as seasons gives us a reminder that it is not permanent. One way or another, it will come to an end. What are some past seasons you have gone through that you thought would never end?

_____

_____

_____

6. God has His own timing and we must learn to trust it. Scripture reminds us to trust God. Read Psalm 31:14-15 and paraphrase it.

_____

_____

_____

7. Are you discouraged by how long it is taking God to answer your prayer? Take this to Him in honest prayer.

_____

_____

_____

8. Re-read the three reasons why we suffer by Swindoll. Is there one you struggle with when you read it? Why?

_____

_____

_____

~ Chapter 5 ~
When Suffering is Unexpected

Christians should not be surprised when they suffer. The previous chapters have shown why no person is immune from it. In fact, Christians should expect another level of suffering.

Beloved, do not be amazed and bewildered at the fiery ordeal which is taking place to test your quality, as though something strange (unusual and alien to you and your position) were befalling you (1 Peter 4:12).

For you have been granted [the privilege] for Christ's sake not only to believe in (adhere to, rely on, and trust in) Him, but also to suffer in His behalf. So you are engaged in the same conflict which you saw me [wage] and which you now hear to be mine [still] (Philippians 1:29-30).

Consider it wholly joyful, my brethren, whenever you are enveloped in or encounter trials of any sort or fall into various temptations. Be assured and understand that the trial and proving of your faith bring out endurance and steadfastness and patience (James 1:2-3).

When I felt God calling me to get to know Him, I was clueless as to what being a Christian was really about. I'd never known anyone who lived a Christ-centered life. When God worked through the hardness of my heart and my belief in Him grew from little or nothing to over 50 percent, my life on earth and my eternal destination changed. I was now past the point where doubt was greater than faith. (I often wonder what that one faith "snowflake" was that caused the momentum to forever shift on my faith balance.)

When my heart and mind accepted Him as my Lord and Leader, heaven cheered and Satan screamed. I was not a threat to Satan as an atheist. I was serving him by believing in myself. Unbeknownst to me, his hatred for me would be shown most through those who were closest to me, and this persecution/suffering (in my case, verbal) would last for decades. Yet, this persecution should have been expected, and it is something I do warn new Christians about so they are not surprised.

If the world hates you, know that it hated Me before it hated you. If you belonged to the world, the world would treat you with affection and would love you as its own. But because you are not of the world [no longer one with it], but I have chosen (selected) you out of the world, the world hates (detests) you (John 15:18-19).

Charles Stanley speaks of this persecution in his book *Finding Peace* and reminds the believer of his/her Helper:

The followers of Jesus are not immune from the circumstances that are trying or disturbing. The promise to them is that the Holy Spirit is present to help, so a problem need not throw them off base or into a tailspin. [The Holy Spirit] speaks peace to the human heart, assuring the believer, 'I'm here. I'm still in charge. Nothing is beyond my strength of my understanding. I'm with you. Don't be afraid.'

How can we **reframe** those unexpected moments, or seasons, of suffering so that we can be open to letting the Holy Spirit work within us?

1) We remind ourselves that God, who never forgets us, is up to something when he sends or allows difficulties to touch us.
2) We put effort into increasing our trust and faith through the storm since nothing touches us until it has come through God.
3) We choose to be thankful that He will supply all our needs. (See Phil 4:19) Of course, we need to remember that only He knows what we really need.
4) We relax in knowing that He is in control and there is nothing too awful or impossible for Him to take care of in our lives—or this world. See Luke 1:37.

5) We observe and act on what is in our circle of control and cast the rest to God. We use it as an opportunity to live actively, yet also being still in His presence.
6) We celebrate the ability to feel pain. Without pain we would not know joy. It is part of our life. Without pain, we would not know that something is wrong with our body, relationships, etc.

In the midst of our agony, we can forget that there is something greater: the joy of the Lord!

God is in control, and the joy of the Lord is going to emerge far greater than any depth of agony we may be experiencing. Our God is a great and limitless God. He dwells in eternity and operates in infinity. He has all things within His understanding and all things under His control (Charles Stanley, Finding Peace*).*

CHAPTER 5: REFLECTION PROMPTS

1. Go back and read through the fifth chapter.

   (a) Write the points of interest.

   _____

   _____

   _____

   (b) Note the Scripture references.

   _____

   _____

   _____

   (c) List any questions you have on the topic of suffering being unexpected that the text did not answer or is leading you to research further.

   _____

   _____

   _____

2. Have you suffered for Christ's sake? Have you experienced any type of persecution for your faith?

   _____

   _____

   _____

3. Re-read James 1:1-3. What three things can trials and the proving of your faith bring about?

   _____

_____

_____

4. Unfortunately, bitterness is often the result of persecution. Do you have any bitterness toward those who have belittled you (or worse) because of your faith?

_____

_____

_____

5. What, if any, physical pain are you experiencing right now? Write down a prayer of thanks for that pain. Can you find 5 things to be thankful for surrounding that pain?

_____

_____

_____

6. Be honest. Do you struggle with the fact that there are non-Christians who are very healthy? Don't seem to struggle financially? Live long lives?

_____

_____

_____

7. Read 2 Peter 1:3. What does God provide to those who love and know Him?

_____

_____

8. Which of the six reframing tips will you adopt to help you walk through the suffering in your life?

_____

_____

_____

~ Chapter 6 ~
Navigating Troubled Waters

When we navigate troubled waters, God is the master of not only the waves, but also the ship (David Jeremiah, When Your World Falls Apart*).*

As I write this chapter, the news is reporting on the Coronavirus and our lives are being impacted with stay-at-home orders and closed, non-essential businesses. It is always worrisome and sad to watch the numbers of people who are sick and dying increase. I know my thoughts immediately go to past plagues that killed millions. Books and movies have made tons of money scaring and freaking people out. But, as Christians, we need to put the past, present, and future disasters and tragedies into their proper perspective.

Nothing is outside of [God's] control. Think about every kind of disaster that terrifies humanity. Every one you name is subject to the God who perseveres. Bad things do happen, but they happen within His supervision and long term purposes. It's foolish to believe things have gotten out of HIs control, it simply cannot happen (David Jeremiah, When Your World Falls Apart*).*

When the Christ-follower navigates the troubled waters of painful experiences, he/she must remember that God gave His permission and that it comes surrounded by His love and will. Nothing happens randomly. God tells us that He is working in all things. Christians should never see hardship as 'bad luck.' God is doing great things, and it would be foolish to think we would ever understand it all.

Jeremiah further reminds us in his book that "there is nothing, no circumstance, no trouble, no testing that can ever touch me until, first of all, it has come past God and past Christ, right through to me. **If it has come that far, it has come with great purpose.**"

When He got into the boat, His disciples followed Him. And suddenly a violent storm arose on the sea, so that the boat was being covered by the waves; but Jesus was sleeping. And the disciples went and woke Him, saying, "Lord, save us, we are going to die!" He said to them, "Why are you afraid, you men of little faith?" Then He got up and rebuked the winds and the sea, and there was [at once] a great and wonderful calm [a perfect peacefulness] (Matthew 8:23-26).

I love how Matt Chandler puts our hurts and circumstances beyond our control into perspective in his book *To Live is Christ; To Die is Gain*:

Since everything is God's, if God wants something, what could you possibly do to stop Him from getting it? For instance, if He wants your life, what are you going to do, eat spinach and go do Pilates? Go ahead and good luck with that. All you have to do is hop online, and you can find somewhere in the world a guy who died today even though he ran marathons and never ate anything but chicken and vegetables. And he was in his thirties...It's all His.

Chandler goes on to remind believers that God doesn't show up and assess or try to fix emergency situations. He is already there and already knows everything. This knowledge can help those suffering troubled waters because it reminds them that they are never alone. For myself, I need to speak very clearly—sometimes audibly— to get the truth of a situation into my head. I am a very emotional person and struggle with turning down the negative and reasoning side of my brain. Having a go-to set of important reminders helps me to focus.

Words worth memorizing and repeating in times of trouble:
* God's got this.
* I am not alone.
* God knows everything.
* God is my protector.
* My life is always in God's hands.
* I am on this earth until He desires I be with Him.
* God can turn all things to good when I trust.
* God is blessing me here and will reward me in eternity.
* God has all power, victory, and majesty—for all is His.
* God always goes before me. I need not flinch or fear. I need not dwell in depression or be anxious.
* God cares about me and everything concerning me.
* God comforts me.
* God is meeting my needs.

* There is no problem God can't handle.
* God is in control.
* I will have more joy in the Lord after this.
* God's love is stronger than any agony.
* God is limitless.
* Bad things do not surprise God.
* Nothing can get out of control for God.
* Nothing in my life is random.
* I am not God and don't know everything.
* God walks beside me in all things.
* Nothing touches me without God's permission.
* My past can be used for good in God's kingdom.
* God put His Spirit inside me to guide and comfort me.
* God's Spirit is my Counselor, Helper, and Comforter.
* I can live the abundant life God wants me to have.
* God knows my thoughts and meets me where I am.

CHAPTER 6: REFLECTION PROMPTS

1. Go back and read through the sixth chapter.

   (a) Write the points of interest.

_____

_____

_____

   (b) Note the Scripture references.

_____

_____

_____

   (c) List any questions you have on the topic of navigating troubled waters that the text did not answer or is leading you to research further.

_____

_____

_____

2. How did the Coronavirus outbreak in 2020 affect your family? Were there any positives that came from your experience through the event?

_____

_____

_____

_____

_____

_____

3. Read 2 Corinthians 4:17. How does Paul describe our afflictions? What are our afflictions producing?

_____

_____

_____

4. Pick five from the list of go to words to memorize in times of trouble and write them down. What made you choose those specific ones? Write it all out.

_____

_____

_____

5. Do you know someone who is young or lives a healthy lifestyle and is struggling with sickness? Take that person to God in prayer and thank Him that He is in control and cares what happens to each person—those who love Him and those who need Him.

_____

_____

_____

6. What negative thought is constantly ruminating in your mind? Take this to God.

_____

_____

_____

~ Chapter 7 ~
Benefits of Suffering

LEARNING TO TRUST

By our choices, we can keep some dangers—like consequences—from coming our way, but not everything. And sudden and personal tragedies can provide opportunities that would not have otherwise crossed our paths. It is in our tragedies that we realize our need for help, comfort, and guidance. Charles Stanley put it this way in his book *Finding Peace:*

It is at this very point of need that our kind and loving God can open the window to our hearts. When we give the okay, God will come to our rescue. He does this by helping us understand His plan. So, God's plan is for all of us—in every generation and in every nation—to ask for His mercy, confess our sins, and trust him for our salvation.

A wonderful aspect of trust is that it can be grown in the good times and in the bad because God can be trusted in the good times and in the bad. Growth happens in the sunshine and in the rain. Try taking moments amidst suffering to remind yourself to trust. See the moments of not getting what you want as opportunities to remind yourself that God is never too big to care and that we are never too small to be cared about.

My help comes from the Lord, Who made heaven and earth (Psalm 121:2).

The Lord is your keeper; the Lord is your shade on your right hand [the side not carrying a shield]. The sun shall not smite you by day, nor the moon by night. The Lord will keep you from all evil; He will keep your life (Psalm 121:5-7).

GROWING IN WISDOM

We can be very stubborn creatures who don't learn easily. God can use suffering to help us see the errors in our past choices and behavior. He provides guidance in our days when we are paying attention and not ignoring them.

Life is hard, but it is in the hard times that we grow in wisdom. The most precious revelations in my own life revolved around pain, hurt, betrayal, and the unknown. We rarely receive anything of worth without a price.

One of the wisest things we can do is go to God and ask for His help and admit that we can't do anything without Him. Our struggles decrease and are less magnified when we invite His presence into them. He can make hard things easier and bring peace out of frustration.

For the Lord gives skillful and godly Wisdom; from His mouth come knowledge and understanding (Proverbs 2:6).

LESS ANXIETY

How can enduring suffering help us to have less anxiety? Suffering can drive us to God. As my suffering increased, my relationship with God grew closer. I read more of His Word, listened to more wise teachings, and often evaluated my circumstances in light of God's sovereignty. This is the beauty of suffering and it helped me to have less anxiety in those times and, in turn, less suffering and anxiety in similar events in the future. With each situation, I was able to apply more of the wisdom God was placing in me.

...Why should we be troubled and lose our peace if we remember our Lord's example of living confidently knowing that His Father was watching, directing, caring for, and loving Him and His followers on a daily basis. God will do the same for us (Charles Stanley, Finding Peace).

INCREASED GRATITUDE

Matt Chandler wrote, "The true test of maturity of our faith would be whether we were prepared to engage in thanksgiving if it had ended terribly. Could we praise if there was loss? Amidst suffering, we are reminded of, and thankful for, God's attentive ear and caring heart to all our prayers."

However, Chandler went on to clarify that "this is not about being thankful for the loss. It is about being thankful for having had the gift. It is about remembering that God is good and that He does good. That He gives and takes away and at all times His name is and should be blessed."

Taking our prayers (which increase during suffering) to God thereby increases our thanksgiving. That, in turn, decreases our anxiety—maybe even to the point of vanishing because thanksgiving and peace have filled up the space that held the anxiety.

INNER CALM

No one can escape God's presence and believers who know this truth can walk in confidence and be content.

Though I walk in the midst of trouble, You will revive

me; You will stretch forth Your hand against the wrath of my enemies, and Your right hand will save me (Psalm 138:7).

Where could I go from Your Spirit? Or where could I flee from Your presence? (Psalm 139:7)

Inner calm can increase, but it requires stepping back and viewing the suffering from a Christian worldview. God's family will go through storms in this life. Yet, it is while going through the storms that God's peace becomes most evident.

Do not fret or have any anxiety about anything, but in every circumstance and in everything, by prayer and petition (definite requests), with thanksgiving, continue to make your wants known to God. And God's peace [shall be yours, that tranquil state of a soul assured of its salvation through Christ, and so fearing nothing from God and being content with its earthly lot of whatever sort that is, that peace] which transcends all understanding shall garrison and mount guard over your hearts and minds in Christ Jesus (Philippians 4:6-7).

A note of warning: Many of my favorite mentors I have mentioned in this book speak of the peace, the inner calm, and the lack of anxiety that believers have once they are grounded in the awareness of being in God's hands. It often sounds like this peace should be automatic, and I find myself feeling inadequate and a complete failure in my walk because I still struggle in these areas. Perhaps there are people that have felt the disappearance of anxiety as soon as they accepted Christ, prayed, or have had people pray for them. Unfortunately, that is not my testimony, but God is not shocked. He knows my testimony and He has a purpose for it.

I encourage you, if you struggle as I have with anxiety, to not give up, to not let yourself feel unworthy, or to label yourself as a failure. Press on. Sanctification—growing in Christ-likeness—requires time and effort. Focus on how far you have come in your walk and where you are going. Do not compare yourself with others. Take who you are to God and let Him mold you into who you are meant to be.

GREATER COURAGE

Life's problems, in [the non-believer] are random and meaningless...The believer encounters the same problem, but he summons up the courage to face it because he knows that within every seemingly random event, God injects a purpose. (David Jeremiah, God Loves You)

We can announce to our problem, sickness, or situation that it can't do anything to us that God, who breathed life into us, does not allow. He controls the number of our days. This leads to courage and peace that passes understanding.

The benefits of suffering don't end here, there are more…

CHAPTER 7: REFLECTION PROMPTS

1. Go back and read through the seventh chapter.

    (a) Write the points of interest.

    _____

    _____

    _____

    (b) Note the Scripture references.

    _____

    _____

    _____

    (c) List any questions you have on the topic of the benefits of suffering that the text did not answer or is leading you to research further.

    _____

    _____

    _____

2. Reflecting back on a suffering that ended well in your own life, how do you think you would have handled it had it not ended well?

_____

_____

_____

_____

_____

_____

3. Reflecting back on a suffering that did not end the way you had hoped, have you found thanksgiving and gratitude in that experience?

_____

_____

_____

4. Do you feel like a failure when you struggle with things that come easier to others? Why?

_____

_____

_____

5. What do you have anxiety about right now? Take it to God with thanksgiving.

_____

_____

_____

6. Write a paragraph directly to your problem and announce to it that it can't do anything to you that God, who breathed life into you, does not allow.

_____

_____

_____

_____

7. Read Proverbs 4:5. When you finish this book, have a plan ready for your next steps in getting more skillful and Godly wisdom. Write it out.

_____

_____

_____

_____

_____

_____

~ Chapter 8 ~
Suffering as a Friend

NOTE: The intent of this book is to help deal with the general suffering all of us will face in our life: sickness, pain, betrayal, death, consequences of our actions, etc. If your suffering was or is due to abuse (such as mental, physical, sexual, or verbal abuse as a child), you may be very irritated just to read the title of this chapter. However, I want to encourage you to listen to Joyce Meyer's messages. She suffered from sexual and verbal abuse from her father for years and is a great example of getting through such tragedies with power and hope, and eventually seeing purpose in everything she went through. I pray this book is a springboard in the healing process for you.

In my own life, my suffering usually leads me down the road of complaining/self-pity, or the road of prayer. It is the common struggle between our flesh and our spirit.

For I do not understand my own actions [I am baffled, bewildered]. I do not practice or accomplish what I wish, but I do the very thing that I loathe [which my moral instinct condemns] (Romans 7:15).

But our go-to in any suffering should be prayer.

Is anyone among you afflicted (ill-treated, suffering evil)? He should pray. Is anyone glad at heart? He should sing praise [to God] (James 5:13).

If you have read almost any of the New Testament, you are aware of the suffering that Paul went through. Yet it is clear from his words, that he was grateful for the suffering and persecution. He counted it as joy and a blessing, just as James, Jesus' brother, encourages us to do:

Consider it wholly joyful, my brethren, whenever you are enveloped in or encounter trials of any sort or fall into various temptations. Be assured and understand that the trial and proving of your faith bring out endurance and steadfastness and patience (James 1:2-3).

What if we had a paradigm shift, based on God's Word, on how we looked at our suffering? What if we viewed it as a friend and not an enemy? A step on the way to our potential?

Before I was afflicted I went astray, but now Your Word do I keep [hearing receiving, loving, and obeying it] (Psalm 119:67).

72

For me to live is Christ [His life in me]. And to die is gain [the gain of the glory of eternity] (Philippians 1:21).

John Ortberg, in his book *The Me I Want to Be*, wrote, "Is it possible that in some way people actually need adversity, setbacks, maybe even something like trauma to reach the fullest level of development and growth?" God, at all times, knows what we need to be and who He made us to be. Why do we trust that He sent His Son to redeem us, but not that He is aware of what we are going through and why? If we want what God wants for us, then we need to trust His love even in the hard times. What if we welcome what He allows as a type of friend?

David Jeremiah stated, "Nothing is meaningless in the world of the believer. Everything has purpose, and in a world ruled by a loving God, the purpose is always to use every encounter to shape us into the perfect image of our Lord."

And we know that all things work together for good to those who love God, to those who are called according to His purpose. For who He foreknew, He also predestined to be conformed to the image of His Son, that He might be the firstborn among many brethren (Romans: 8:28-29).

Since there is no guarantee that God will remove the difficult circumstances in our lives, we can learn to suffer well and discover the good in it all. Matt Chandler reminded readers of this in his book *To Live is Christ, To Die is Gain*: "It isn't wrong to ask God to relieve you of your pain, but it is more important that in the midst of the pain you rely on the promise of God to work such experiences for His glory and your good—to use these times as a means of perfecting your faith, strengthening your spirit, and transforming your life in such a way that you are becoming more like Jesus."

We must stay balanced when it comes to being grateful for suffering. We do not want to go to the extreme where we seek to have horrible things happen. He is glorified when we maintain our hope in Him despite the suffering. He is glorified when we notice what He is doing in our lives instead of focusing on what He is not doing. He is glorified when we remember that He not only knows what is going on, but He already knows the outcomes of our sufferings. We can rest in the confidence that He has a good plan.

CHAPTER 8: REFLECTION PROMPTS

1. Go back and read through the eighth chapter.
   (a) Write the points of interest.

   _____

   _____

   _____

   (b) Note the Scripture references.

   _____

   _____

   _____

   (c) List any questions you have on the topic of suffering as a friend that the text did not answer or is leading you to research further.

   _____

   _____

   _____

2. Was there a suffering in your life that brought you closer to God?

_____

_____

_____

3. Do you struggle with prayer and being consistent in your time with God when you are suffering?

_____

_____

_____

4. Is there anything in your life that seems meaningless right now? Can you imagine a way God is going to use this to shape you into His image?

_____

_____

_____

5. Each act of obedience is a type of worship. Read the book of Esther and notice how she was willing to lay aside her plan and accept God's plan—even though she did not understand it.

_____

_____

_____

6. Do you have pity-parties? Explain why they are a waste of time and imagine what God thinks of them.

_____

_____

_____

7. Read Jeremiah 29:11. God's plan is a possibility, not a positively. We need to choose to cooperate with God, develop our gifts and talents, and not stray from His will.

What is a simple action step you can take to cooperate with God today?

_____

_____

_____

~ Chapter 9 ~
Suffering Increases Strength

And after you have suffered a little while, the God of all grace [Who imparts all blessing and favor], Who has called you to His [own] eternal glory in Christ Jesus, will Himself complete and make you what you ought to be, establish and ground you securely, and strengthen, and settle you (1 Peter 5: 10).

Suffering and strength are two sides of the same coin. (David Jeremiah, When Your World Falls Apart).

My children are teenagers, and I see them making poor decisions occasionally and suffering from the consequences. My job is to step in and guide them through the situation. My hope is that they grow from the experience. An important part of their growth will be via the sufferings they go through. In my own life, I can look back at some of the stupid decisions I made in my teens and twenties and see the growth that came from those moments.

God sends trouble into our lives to strengthen us and make us better children in His family (David Jeremiah).

Putting suffering into perspective instead of trying to run from it is how we strengthen our relationship with Christ and demonstrate our faith in Him to others. Again, we are not running toward pain or looking for it, but we are taking advantage of what is given.

Believers can faithfully endure suffering and remain steadfast amidst the trials in life. When we experience difficulties and discouragement, we can focus on Christ and endure without complaint (or less complaining as we mature) and have patience and perseverance.

If then you have been raised with Christ [to a new life, thus sharing His resurrection from the dead], aim at and seek the [rich eternal treasures] that are above, where Christ is, seated at the right hand of God. And set your minds and keep them set on what is above (the higher things), not on the things that are on the earth (Colossians 3:1-2).

The benefits of suffering are found not only in ourselves, but also in our circle of influence. Perseverance and strength amidst suffering is seen by others. We can become someone's safe place to talk about situations and how it made us better people in God's Kingdom. We can share our testimony and help others who go through a similar situation in the future. Our suffering has given us wisdom and maturity. It has given us perspective and perseverance. We can now take that strength and share it with other people. People will see us thanking God for what we went through and want to be that same strong person on the other side of their own problem.

Trees get a part of their strength by enduring the wind. We get a part of our strength by enduring suffering. God doesn't want us focusing on the suffering (circumstances), He wants us focusing on our relationship with Him and being the person He created you and me to be.

God has plans to use our suffering in ways only He knows. If He allows, we will have eyes to see the increased strength from our times of suffering, but we need to be looking. Our focus needs to begin not with our suffering, but with Christ—He is our true strength! (Joyce Meyer)

King David is a great example of one who trusted in the strength of God to give him the strength he needed:

Both riches and honor come from You, and You reign over all. In Your hands are power and might; in Your hands it is to make great and to give strength to all (1 Chronicles 29:12).

And Moses reminded Joshua, the next leader of Israel, to

not fear for:

It is the Lord Who goes before you; He will [march] with you; He will not fail you or let you go or forsake you; [let there be no cowardice or flinching, but] fear not, neither become broken [in spirit—depressed, dismayed, and unnerved with alarm] (Deuteronomy 31:8).

Can we be confident that whatever comes upon us will be beneficial to us in some way? David Jeremiah, in his book *God Loves You*, would say yes: "As more than conquerors, whatever comes against us actually ends up working in our favor. Every difficulty that challenges us finally serves to prove the love of God, from which nothing can separate us."

Yet amid all these things we are more than conquerors and gain a surpassing victory through Him Who loved us (Romans 8:37).

Suffering in the present may be exactly what we need to prepare us for the future. Only God knows, and we may not see the benefits for years, decades, or on this side of heaven. This is when we need to trust our Lord and lean on Him.

Our suffering may be completely unexpected and so tragic that it seems without purpose: the loss of a healthy spouse, the sickness of a child, the loss of a child, etc. I cannot imagine the pain felt by such experiences. But I do know that I will have loss in the future, and studying suffering and seeing the good in my previous sufferings will prepare my heart and soul for that difficult time.

In the midst of these horrible moments, a believer's strength and trust in God will waiver in some measure. If it doesn't, then that believer may want to write a book of their own—I am sure it could help many. If our strength and trust were measured, however, I believe one who has learned from, grown in, and benefited via past sufferings will see greater strength and trust in future episodes of suffering.

Chuck Swindoll wrote, in his book *Living the Proverbs*, this great reminder: "God never wastes our time. He doesn't allow us to go through dark and dismal valleys or endure those long, winding, and painful paths for no reason."

CHAPTER 9: REFLECTION PROMPTS

1. Go back and read through the ninth chapter.

   (a) Write the points of interest.

_____

_____

_____

   (b) Note the Scripture references.

_____

_____

_____

   (c) List any questions you have on the topic of how suffering increases strength that the text did not answer or is leading you to research further.

_____

_____

_____

2. "After you have suffered a little while..." Peter says. Read 1 Peter 5:6-11. Who else is going to suffer? How long is a "little while?"

_____

_____

_____

3. Do you have children? Do you struggle with letting them suffer the consequences of their actions?

_____

_____

_____

4. Are you an example of steadfastness and faith to others amidst suffering? Note a couple of action steps you can take to improve in this area.

_____

_____

_____

5. Not knowing why something is happening can be very frustrating. What does Peter say we need to do with our anxiety in 1 Peter 5:7?

_____

_____

_____

6. Name something you have endured that has made you stronger. Have you had the opportunity to share what you learned with another who is going through the same thing?

_____

_____

_____

7. The author of Hebrews reminds us that God will never fail us or leave us without support. Therefore, we are to be satisfied with what? Read Hebrews 13:5.

_____

_____

_____

8. Sometimes God needs to prune us to get us to a new level. Pruning can be painful and not always understood. Are you being pruned right now? Are you abiding in Christ? Read John 5.

_____

_____

_____

9. God delights in our spiritual growth. He does not delight in our suffering. When has the strength of your faith increased the most? When everything was good or bad?

_____

_____

_____

~ Chapter 10 ~

Suffering Gets Our Attention

God sends the storm to force us to look for Christ walking on the waves (David Jeremiah, When Your World Falls Apart*).*

For the Christ-follower, nature is just another part of creation. Therefore, it is controlled by God. In every dark day that we experience, we can be thankful that there is always hope, joy, and an opportunity to see God keeping His promises. The only person who can help us perfectly when the dark days come upon us is God. He describes Himself as our rock, fortress, hope, and confidence.

Although most, if not all, suffering will get our attention, it is how we respond to it that determines if we will come out the other side stronger/better or angry/bitter. Fire purifies, and it is the same with suffering. It is when we are "squeezed" that we see what is living on the inside. We have the free will to choose how we respond to the good and bad that God is allowing to bring about His purposes.

Joyce Meyer, in her *Everyday Life Bible*, wrote, "God does not delight in our suffering, but He is honored and pleased when we endure it with a good attitude. Trust requires unanswered questions. If we knew all the answers, faith would not even be necessary."

We get to choose if we want to waste our opportunities for growth. Each moment is filled with numerous thoughts and possible decisions to lead us down a path toward becoming a stronger and more refined child of God—if we recognize them. How we behave during trials is a true test of faith, especially when the trial seems unfair.

Few of us ever fully grasp the simple but painful biblical truth: the heat of suffering is a refining fire purifying the gold of godly character and wisdom… God often uses the tools of suffering and affliction to sanctify us. These trials function like a fire that burns off every impurity impeding our progress toward holiness (David Jeremiah, God Loves You*).*

Since God does allow suffering to bring about His purposes, it is important that we remember that He allows them only for a time in the life of the believer. True, that amount of time is unknown to us, but He loves us and does not give us more than we can bear. The Amplified Version of 1 Corinthians 10:13 further "amplifies" this important Scripture:

For no temptation (no trial regarded as enticing to sin), [no matter how it comes or where it leads] has overtaken you and laid hold on you that is not common to man [that is, no temptation or trial has come to you that is beyond human resistance and that is not adjusted and adapted and belonging to human experience, and such as man can bear. But God is faithful] to His Word and to His compassionate nature, and He [can be trusted] not to let you be tempted and tried and assayed beyond your ability and strength of resistance and power to endure, but with the temptation He will [always] also provide the way out (the means of escape to a landing place), that you may be capable and strong and powerful to bear up under it patiently.

Personal: Are all of my documents in order for my kids: will, medical releases, funeral preferences, and wishes for my tangible property?

Business: Will my businesses function smoothly without me? Are all the tasks I do fully redundant and able to be taken care of by someone else?

Legacy: What will people say about me at my funeral? Is there time to change, restore, fix, or make amends to struggling relationships?

Taxes: Is everything setup to go into my trust to avoid probate? Are the cars and the house setup to transfer on death to my spouse?

Paperwork: Does my family know where all of the important documents in my life are located? Passwords? Taxes? Military documents?

Goods: How much of my stuff am I leaving for my family to sort through? Can I give any of it away now?

Time: What do I want to do with the time I have remaining in my life?

Projects: Is there a project I have been putting off and I can now do because I have extra time waiting in hospital rooms, resting as the doctor ordered, or taking time away from work?

Memoir: Have I written down the events, blessings, and lessons learned for my posterity?

Creativity: Do I have time to write the novel I want to write? Did I get all my creative works copyrighted? Should I publish a work on my own or get help?

Past: Was there something I did in the past that, over time, has allowed the situation I am in to exist? Is there someone I can help by sharing this lesson with them?

Holiness: Is God trying to teach me something? Is there an area of sin in my life right now that I have not acknowledged or dealt with?

Fear: Am I afraid of dying? Why?

Trust: Am I really trusting God?

Prayer: Is God hearing my prayers?

Action: Is there anything I can do, that I refuse to do that can help me in this situation?

Pride: Am I too prideful to let my friends know that I need prayer and that I am struggling?

Hope: Is there any hope in this situation? Is it going to get worse?

Gratitude: What else can I be grateful for? What am I ignoring?

Sometimes the situations we would like to avoid are the most profitable circumstances we go through (Charles Stanley, Finding Peace*).*

CHAPTER 10: REFLECTION PROMPTS

1. Go back and read through the tenth chapter.

(a) Write the points of interest.

_____

_____

_____

(b) Note the Scripture references.

_____

_____

_____

(c) List any questions you have on the topic of suffering gets our attention that the text did not answer or is leading you to research further.

_____

_____

_____

2. Read Zechariah 9:12. We should never stop hoping in God. What does this verse encourage us to be?

_____

_____

_____

3. Facing a crisis can motivate us to tackle the concerns it raises. If you were to die tomorrow, what thoughts enter

your mind? Make your own list and pick a couple of items to take care of over the next month.

_____

_____

_____

4. How has suffering in the past made you a better person?

_____

_____

_____

5. God does not delight in our suffering yet He allows it in our lives. How do you feel about that? Can you think of a situation where you would allow suffering in a child's life and not delight in it?

_____

_____

_____

6. God's presence can eliminate much of the struggle we experience, but you need to invite Him in. Is there something you have not asked Him for help with?

_____

_____

_____

7. Read Hebrews 13:6. What are you afraid of, dreading, or terrified by? Confidently take it to your Helper.

_____

_____

_____

~ Chapter 11 ~
Profiting from Suffering

Whatever struggle or setback you face is intended to empower and purify you. (David Jeremiah, When Your World Falls Apart*)*

The way we respond to the suffering God allows is the driving force as to whether or not it will be profitable to us. Whatever we go through does not automatically result in us being a better version of ourselves. We often see the reverse result: sadness can lead to drinking, pain can lead to addiction, stress can lead to overeating, etc.

Seeing the profit in any suffering can be blocked by the suffering itself. Therefore, it is important to go to God first before going to the world for answers, then go to godly friends and family for comfort and guidance. One of my favorite ways to pray is to journal a conversation directly with God on whatever I am going through. I believe, with God's Spirit within me, I am able to bypass the fleshly, worried part of me and see God's words in my own hand. Here is a very simple example of this type of conversational prayer from my own journal:

Father, I got so angry with my husband last night for not stepping in when the kids were being disrespectful to me. In fact, this has been going on for years. It's like he really doesn't hear what is going on around him or doesn't care.

Have you calmly asked him for help? His advice? Beloved, you know you can't change your husband and he can't read your mind. I must do the changing within him, and he must be a partaker in that growth. You fear you are failing as a mother. Give that over to me—your children as well.

Lord, I am so tired. I feel like giving up on so many things— disciplining the kids, moderating the electronics, homeschooling. I know it is not right. I feel so pitiful.

Daughter, you are frustrated and confused. You are expecting perfection. Your kids are thriving, learning, and they need your guidance and discipline. Do what you can do, and give the rest to me.

Thank you, God. Please fill me with ideas to help the kids grow into the adults you want them to be.

Cast your cares to me. I am here.

Part of the reason God allows us to experience sorrow and trials in this life is so we might learn that God has the power to sustain us and provide for us all things that produce earthly blessings and eternal benefits. We must truly believe that He is totally capable of handling all things according to the fullness of His plan and purpose for our life. (Charles Stanley, Finding Peace*)*

We can be confident because God is in control. We can move forward in that confidence and trust God to bring about the best of every circumstance. Perhaps, if you have prayed and have not been healed, God has plans to use you and *your* suffering to be an encouragement to someone else. To watch your suffering help someone in their suffering is priceless.

The book of Ruth is a great example of how faith amidst suffering profits not only the person experiencing it, but also others. She suffered loss and was rewarded with being part of the lineage of Christ—which benefited us all. David Jeremiah, author of *When Your World Falls Apart*, wrote, "The moment we accept the fact that our ordeal has been permitted, even intended by God, our perspective on disruptive moments will totally change."

For we are God's [own] handiwork (His workmanship), recreated in Christ Jesus, [born anew] that we may do those good works which God predestined (planned before hand) for us [taking paths which He prepared ahead of time], that we should walk in them [living the good life which He prearranged and made ready for us to live] (Ephesians 3:10).

We can praise God in the midst of our pain, trials, and sorrow. We can be honest with Him about our hurt and frustration. We can bring Him our tears and still praise and love Him.

Search me [thoroughly], O God, and know my heart! Try me and know my thoughts! And see if there is any wicked or hurtful way in me, and lead me in the way everlasting (Psalm 139: 23-24).

I will praise You, for I am fearfully and wonderfully made; Marvelous are Your works, And that my soul knows very well (Psalm 139: 14, NKJV).

My dad drilled into me the famous saying, "It is your attitude not your aptitude that will get you to your altitude." It is the same with suffering. With God's clarity of the situation or without, our view of our suffering can make all the difference for us and others. We can choose to smile and trust, be grateful and praise, and pray with hopefulness. The choice is ours. We have the opportunity to make the worst thing that ever happened to us into the best thing that could have ever happened.

CHAPTER 11: REFLECTION PROMPTS

1. Go back and read through the eleventh chapter.
   (a) Write the points of interest.

   _____
   _____
   _____

   (b) Note the Scripture references.

   _____
   _____
   _____

   (c) List any questions you have on the topic of profiting from suffering that the text did not answer or is leading you to research further.

   _____
   _____
   _____

2. Attitude check? How is it today? This week? This year?

   _____
   _____
   _____

3. Take your attitude thoughts and do a conversational prayer with God in your journal.

   _____
   _____

_____

4. Take something you are waiting for God to restore in your life and begin to thank Him for restoring it in His way and in His timing.

_____

_____

_____

5. Being kind to others helps us overcome the pain and disappointments we experience. It also helps release joy in our own lives. Do something kind for someone today.

_____

_____

_____

6. Read the book of Ruth. It is short and powerful.

_____

_____

_____

7. Ruth suffered great loss, but her life was not over. She stepped out and moved forward. Is there a step you can take to move forward into the next season of your life?

_____

_____

~ Chapter 12 ~
Suffering Brings Clarity

Sometimes we can only see what is in us when we are "squeezed." Is love, joy, prayer, and trust coming from you when you endure difficult times? Or is anger, hate, irritation, and frustration coming out? We are human, and as Christ-followers we are in the sanctification process. Therefore, we should all be growing in our Christ-likeness year after year. Bottom line: the "product" you release when you are squeezed after knowing Christ for ten years should not be the same "product" you released when you were squeezed a couple of years after knowing Christ.

So, our suffering shows our progress in our walk with God. Matt Chandler wrote, "Mature faith is always rejoicing." If I may take his quote and alter it slightly, based on what I have learned, I would say: Maturing faith learns to rejoice more and more in any given circumstance.

David Jeremiah, in his book *God Loves You*, wrote, "Where do we get the idea that God has promised us an easy ride through life? Not from Scripture; it's not there."
We grow up hearing stories of happy endings, but that is rarely how life works. God gives us what He knows we

need, but it is not always what we want. Don't forget, we are supposed to count all these trials as joyful.

Consider it wholly joyful, my brethren, whenever you are enveloped in or encounter trials of any sort or fall into various temptations. Be assured and understand that the trial and proving of your faith bring out endurance and steadfastness and patience (James 1:2-3).

This is the most repeated verse in this book because it is the most important, in my opinion, when it comes to difficult situations. Sometimes healing is not God's plan on this side of heaven. However, we don't know this and so we should never give up hope, trust, prayer, and confidence. We can be faithful and trusting even if the healing doesn't come. Know that God does not delight in our suffering or death, and it does not come to pass unless He allows it.

For the Lord will not cast off forever! But though He causes grief, yet will He be moved to compassion according to the multitude of His loving-kindness and tender mercy. For He does not willingly and from His heart afflict or grieve the children of men (Lamentations 3:32-33).

Who is he who speaks and it comes to pass, if the Lord

has not authorized and commanded it? Is it not out of the mouth of the Most High that evil and good both proceed [adversity and prosperity, physical evil or misfortune and physical good or happiness]? (Lamentations 3:37-38)

Billy Graham, in his book *Where I Am*, wrote, "I cannot find anywhere in Scripture that promises one more minute of life." We are rarely going to agree with the timing of our own suffering. It reminds me of people who are waiting to be ready to be parents. No one is ever perfectly ready. But there are things a couple can do to prepare: pray, save money, evaluate time, complete activities that take considerable effort and resources.

And so it is with people and suffering. We will suffer and we won't be perfectly ready, but we can prepare: **grow in our relationship with Christ, stay in communication with God regularly (prayer), study God's Word, be part of a healthy family of believers at a local church, have our affairs in order, and read books on how God has worked in the lives of others.**

Time is not seen by God the same way we see it. That is why trust is so important. We need to evaluate our attitude during the hard times—they will make or break us. Although we can never know all of God's purposes in our

lives, at times He gives us the perspective to look back at
the low we endured and see the good that came from it.
(David Jeremiah, When Your World Falls Apart*)*

CHAPTER 12: REFLECTION PROMPTS

1. Go back and read through the twelfth chapter.

   (a) Write the points of interest.

   _____

   _____

   _____

   (b) Note the Scripture references.

   _____

   _____

   _____

   (c) List any questions you have on the topic of suffering brings clarity that the text did not answer or is leading you to research further.

   _____

   _____

   _____

2. Ask God to help you see where you need His help in your life when it comes to your suffering.

_____

_____

_____

3. Evaluate yourself honestly by answering the following questions:

Are you angry at God?

_____

_____

Are you running to something other than Him?

_____

_____

Are you trying to escape the pain with food, drinks, relationships, etc?

_____

_____

Have you lost hope?

_____

_____

Are you depressed or anxious?

_____

_____

Have you honestly lifted all your cares to Him?

_____

_____

Are you consumed with your pain and suffering?

_____

_____

Have you forgotten to laugh and love others during this time?

_____

_____

Do you feel like giving up?

_____

_____

Do you think God is not listening?

_____

_____

Are you questioning God's control or timing?

_____

_____

Are you demanding a happy ending?

_____

_____

How do you feel after answering these questions?

_____

_____

_____

_____

_____

_____

_____

Chapter 13

Conclusion

*The message of the Bible is to 'exhort believers to embrace
every circumstance God sends or allows,' even to go as far
as to 'count it all joy' in the hope that God's ultimate
purposes will be fulfilled (Joyce Meyer, The Everyday Life
Bible).*

God has a purpose and a reason for prompting me to write
this book. I don't know the full extent of how He will use it for
His purpose in your life or mine. However, I do know that the
research and writing of this topic was beyond helpful for
getting through some difficulties in my own life.
Difficult situations and suffering will come to everyone. Yet,
the information in this book can help the one going through
suffering right now, the one who will suffer eventually, and
the one who is watching another suffer.

A word of caution: Please apply the teachings in this book
to your own life, or share them with someone who is
seeking purpose and reason in their own suffering. It is, I
believe, unwise and careless to take the words and help in
this book and go to a person who has just lost a loved one
and tell them that: "Everything happens for a reason. God

knows what He is doing." Truth with compassionate timing is important, for grief is a part of life that God fully understands and also comforts us in.

Blessed be the God and Father of our Lord Jesus Christ, the Father of sympathy (pity and mercy) and the God [Who is the Source] of every comfort (consolation and encouragement). Who comforts (consoles and encourages) us in every trouble (calamity and affliction), so that we may also be able to comfort (console and encourage) those who are in any kind of trouble or distress, with the comfort (consolation and encouragement) with which we ourselves are comforted (consoled and encouraged) by God (2 Corinthians 1:3-4).

~ Chapter 14 ~
Next Steps

If you have made it through the book to this chapter, I would imagine you are a seeker and a lover of learning. Therefore, I highly recommend the following steps to continue your journey:

1) Read/Study
2) Pray
3) Fellowship
4) Research
5) Evaluate

Read/Study

Do not conform to the pattern of this world, but be transformed by the renewing of your mind. Then you will be able to test and approve what God's will is—His good, pleasing, and perfect will (Romans 12:2, NIV).

Get a good study Bible. I recommend:

- *The Woman's Study Bible (NKJV)* by Thomas Nelson
- *The Maxwell Leadership Bible* by Thomas Nelson
- *The Joyce Meyer Study Bible (AMP)* by Warner Faith

Study some of the Christian Classics:

- *The Practice of the Presence* of God by Brother Lawrence
- *The Imitation of Christ* by Thomas a Kempis
- *A Practical View of Christianity* by Garth M. Rosell
- *Morning by Morning* by Charles H. Spurgeon
- *Grace Abounding to the Chief of Sinners* by John Bunyan
- *The Kneeling Christian* by Anonymous
- *Plain Account of Christian Perfection* by John Wesley
- *Humility & Absolute Surrender* by Andrew Murray
- *Life in the Spirit* by A.W. Tozer
- *A Practical View of Christianity* by William Wilberforce
- *The Pilgrim's Progress* by John Bunyan

Study books written and recommended by your favorite seasoned, mature Bible teachers. And don't forget their Podcasts! This is how I studied for *Does Everything Happen for a Reason, God?* See References.

Pray

In prayer, our anxiety is reduced, and often resolved, because we are trusting God in that moment. We are bringing the anxiety to the only One Who can handle it.

Fellowship

Attend a good, Bible based church regularly. See Hebrews 10:25. Find a great accountability partner to help you and join a small group or Sunday school class.

Research

Hear something that doesn't sound quite right from a friend, a blog, or your pastor? Don't just brush off that feeling. Research it. Go to God's Word first and then to your trusted Bible teachers and dig into that subject. You may be surprised by how much you learn when you research only one topic.

Evaluate

Personal reflection is a big part of our growth. God gives revelation and we must be willing to evaluate ourselves honestly. Are you a person of peace who seeks to understand? Are you argumentative?

Are you thinking eternally? Have you made a decision about Christ? Have you placed yourself in His hands to be molded as He desires, or have you pushed Him away?

...I have set before you life and death, the blessings and

the curses; therefore choose life, that you and your
descendants may live and may love the Lord your God,
obey His voice, and cling to Him. For He is your life and
the length of your days... (Deuteronomy 30:19b-20a)

Enjoy the journey.

References

Chandler, Matt. (2013). *To live is Christ to die is gain*. David C. Cook.

Graham, Billy. (2015). *Where I am: Heaven, eternity, and our life beyond*. Thomas Nelson.

Jeremiah, David. (2017). *Count it all joy: Discover a happiness that circumstances cannot change*. David C. Cook.

Jeremiah, David. (2014) *God loves you: He always has--he always will*. FaithWords.

Jeremiah, David. (2000). *When your world falls apart: Seeing past the pain of the present*. W Publishing Group.

Meyer, Joyce. (2018). *The everyday life Bible: The power of God's Word for everyday living*. FaithWords.

Meyer, Joyce. (2015). *Let God fight your battles: Being peaceful in the storm*. FaithWords.

Ortberg, John. (2014). *The me I wan to be: Becoming God's*

best version of you. Zondervan.

Stanley, Charles. (2007). *Finding peace: God's promise of a life free from regret, anxiety, and fear.* Thomas Nelson.

Swindoll, Charles. (2013). *Embraced by the Spirit: The untold blessings of intimacy with God.* Worthy Books.

Swindoll, Charles. (2014). *Living the proverbs: Insight for the daily grind.* Worthy Books.

Connect

On the Web: www.LillyHorigan.com

On Facebook: fb.me/lillyhorigan

On Twitter: @LillyHorigan

E-Mail: info@LillyHorigan.com

Via Snail Mail: Lilly Books, PO Box 223, Bolivar, OH, 44612

About the Author

Lilly lives in Bolivar, Ohio, with her husband and two boys. She is originally from Horseheads, New York.

Other Books by Lilly

Paper Treasures

Paige McKinnon has finally graduated high school and is ready to embark on the journey she has been planning for years. Alone, she makes her way to Las Vegas where she hopes to locate her mentally ill and homeless mother. A young woman of faith, Paige uses only the prompting of God's Spirit and advice of her aunt to find a place to stay, work, and search for her mother's whereabouts--but will she find love there as well?

On Twitter: #PaperTreasuresNovel

On Amazon: Kindle & Paperback Versions

Chapter 1 of Paper Treasures

Nevada
June 20th, 2016

Paige McKinnon reached into the McDonald's bag one more time, hoping to find another french fry at the bottom—anything to distract her from her grandmother's last text urging her to reconsider leaving home. She had been on the road for hours since waving goodbye and was incredibly nervous already. The texts only made it worse, but she knew her grandmother was only trying to look out for her.

Paige tried to keep her eyes on the road in between eating, drinking, and setting up her phone to play the next chapter of the audiobook she was listening to. Sometimes she wondered how she got where she was without hitting someone or something. She never seemed to be paying any attention to the road in front of her, not with all the thoughts demanding attention in her head.

She had left early in the morning; early for her anyway. She hoped the eight-hour drive would go quickly—she was thrilled to finally be moving to Vegas! Living in Washington since birth meant there would be major adjustments to the Las Vegas climate, but she was eager to get started on her new life, a life on her own to answer questions she had waited years to ask.

She tried to concentrate on the audiobook and follow along, but her mind was going over every possibility she could think of concerning what could happen when she arrived in Vegas. She paused the book and forced herself to focus on the road a few seconds, and began lifting her anxieties up for the hundredth time that day. *God, please make a way for me to see her. Help me find a place to stay and lead me where you want me.*

Paige felt the anxiety diminish but the anticipation kept it lingering in her soul. She was taking a big risk, and it was a risk that no one was happy about back home. She was leaving her family to seek answers of her own.

She was 18 and finally able to make the decision to go. They understood her desire. They saw how her beautiful blond hair, blue eyes, and strong chin looked like no one else's in the family. They knew she wanted to see the person who gave her those unique features. She wanted to see her mother.

She knew her nose and ears were passed on from her father. She never saw it herself, however. He had died in a car accident when she was two. She didn't know all the details of the accident. Her grandmother had a hard time talking about the death of her son. She raised Paige the best she could and her childhood had been fun and healthy.

Now out of high school, she could finally see her mom and try to make a connection with her. Paige knew her mother was sick and knew that even if her mother had wanted to see her over the years, she couldn't have. There were court orders put in place to make sure there was no contact.

Did her mom even know about the orders?

Did her mom even know about her anymore?

~

After hours of staring at a computer screen, Seth Redding finally left his mom's quilt shop. Her dream would soon open and the merchant software he had chosen for her was almost ready for the big day. He had just finished setting up the system to accept credit cards and sell yards of fabric in any measurement.

It seemed there were a million small things that needed to be done, and a thousand little problems that came up that he had not foreseen. He was happy to help her fulfill this dream, but he would have preferred something a little less technical and financial. Trudy Redding had a gift for putting together fabrics and threads in amazing ways but computers seemed to malfunction with only a few keyboard strokes when she was on them.

Seth made his way to his car, contemplating if he should stop at the grocery store next door. He thought his mother had made a wise decision on where to locate the shop. The small shopping center was on one of the busiest roads in their part of town and not far from the highway. Although the shop was small, it was all his mom desired. It was cozy and inviting. It was a perfect addition to the shopping center, which looked more like a quaint downtown village. The parking lot had what patrons would want—practicality and close proximity. It seemed, to Seth anyway, as if she had taken longer to name the shop than any other decision. She had settled with *Quilts On*.

Seth would never forget how thrilled and giddy his mom was the night she had come up with that name. She thought herself so clever putting two of her favorite things into one name—quilt and son. She even had her sign made up so that the text color was different for the last three letters. He suggested maybe the name was a way of hinting that he should start quilting. She laughed at the idea of ever trying to get him to quilt. Sitting at the dinner table watching her squeal with delight when he gave his approval to the name made Seth chuckle again as he walked to his car. She was easily pleased, and he loved that about her.

Seth's interests didn't include fabric or computers. When he wasn't helping his mom, he played his guitar. He had taught himself with the help of online videos, and was amazed that he had been able to get right into the band at church. They attended a big church in Vegas, and they welcomed new people who were willing to be part of worship. There was a growing Christian population in Vegas, although the world would probably never know it. The news only focused on "Sin City" when events lined up with its sinful reputation. Seth was looking forward to being a positive part of the city.

After mentally going over the to-do list to get his mom up and running for the big opening day in less than a week, he decided to stop at the store and pick up food. His little apartment a few blocks away was just the right size for him, but he ate out most of the time. Sitting in an empty house and having dinner alone was less than exciting.

At just over 22 years old, Seth knew he was not like other guys his age. He had returned from serving 4 years in the Navy, and he wasn't interested in bars, gambling, or meeting a different girl every night. Seth was ready to start the next stage of his life—ready to meet the right girl and, in time, start a family. But first, he needed to figure out what he was going to do to support that future family.

Heading for the beer aisle, he picked up a case from a local brewing company. He only drank occasionally, and when he did, he wanted quality beer. After hours of computer work, and repeating the same instructions over and over again to his mom for what seemed like the simplest of tasks, a beer or two would taste great. He picked up a couple ready-to-eat foods at the deli and headed home.

His apartment was on the third floor of a decent complex only five minutes from his mom's new shop. He'd been there less than two months and the refrigerator was not the only thing that looked empty. He had not brought, nor bought, much furniture. There was no point in going into debt or depleting his savings for a couch or table.

Getting out of the Navy in less than four years without any debt was a miracle. Many service members made a lot of dumb financial decisions that took years to fix. Seth's mom, however, had taught him to make use of everything he had and not to go in debt unless necessary. Sometimes they disagreed on what was necessary.

~

Paige finally made it to Vegas late in the afternoon. She had picked a neighborhood that her aunt had visited once. She recalled the letter in her bag that her Aunt Marie had sent her:

Dearest Paige,
I will, of course, share any details I can with you about your mother. As you already know, the last time I saw my sister was a few years ago. Unfortunately, she was in one of the areas that I would not recommend you frequent without someone with you. Also, after visiting Vegas year after year and looking for her, I have come across a few wonderful neighborhoods that I think would be a great place for you to live, work, and begin your search for her. I have included important maps, a bus schedule, and a little money for you. My email and number are on the back of the map. Call me with any questions I can answer for you.

Love,
Aunt Marie

Paige got off the highway and made her way to the area her Aunt recommended. She passed the bus station and an amazing park. Paige knew it was the park her Aunt had written about in one of the many letters and emails she'd sent over the years. Aunt Marie had once run a Veteran's

Day 11K race there when she and her father, Paige's grandfather, had come to visit her mom.

Paige continued on, all while praying for God's hand to show her where to stop and what to do. The shopping centers were small and unique. It was hard to imagine that the Strip, with all its lights and craziness, was only ten minutes away from this seemingly quiet area.

She drove down the road she had seen on her map numerous times before, but now she looked at the places in light of needing to find a job and a place to live. Paige had only enough money to stay in a hotel for a few days.

Her family couldn't believe she had left without knowing where she was going to stay. Equipped with her phone, a car, and some money, she felt she had all that was needed to handle the journey. Paige trusted that God would lead her where she needed to go. However, the weight of the unknown and realization of what she was doing suddenly pressed down on her.

Ready for a break, she entered the parking lot of a shopping center with a large grocery store. Without a place to live, she couldn't shop for groceries yet, but she could buy some water and a sandwich. She was tired of eating fries and cheeseburgers.

The shopping center, along with the grocery store, had a dry cleaner, a quilt shop, and a pizza place. She noted the walkway that connected the house-like shops and was impressed with the cleanliness and the flower pots hanging along the entire property. Someone cared about this area—not many places have this much attention to detail. Even the parking lot was clean and had numerous lantern-type lights along the rows.

Paige instantly liked the area. She could see why her Aunt had recommended it. After getting out of the car and stretching her legs, Paige scanned the area across the street. Although not as cozy as the side she was on, with its pansies and lanterns, it did have a bank, a flower shop, and a café. Purse in hand, she headed to the grocery store but made sure she passed the quilt shop first.

Paige adored any type of craft store. She was drawn to the colors, ideas, and creative possibilities. She always collected beautiful fabrics and threads for future projects. Although Paige didn't do any traditional quilting, many of the women in her family did. In fact, Aunt Marie had recently made her a quilt for her high school graduation. It was in the back of the car, with the rest of her "life," awaiting a new home.

The quilt shop was directly next to store but didn't seem open. Strange, since it was the middle of a weekday. Deciding to take a quick look, she tried the door. Locked. She moved on toward the grocery store and heard the quilt store door unlock and open. A sweet-looking lady, probably in her fifties and about Paige's 5' 4" height, stepped out.

"Can I help you?"

"I'm sorry. I was just checking to see if you were open."

"We're opening next week. I haven't put a sign out yet. Oh, I should get to that. I'll have my son do that this week. And I should put something in the paper. Oh, why didn't I think of that sooner? And some balloons…" The lady seemed to forget all about Paige standing there and was looking in the window, counting on her fingers, and seemed to be mentally adding items to a list.

Paige didn't feel comfortable just walking away. "I'm sure it will all work out. This looks like a great location. Will you have quilt classes for beginners?"

"Oh, I'm sorry. Yes, yes. We'll have classes for all levels. Have you ever quilted before?"

"No, but I have done some embroidery and cross-stitching in the past."

"Then you'll have to stop by for the beginner's class when it starts, probably in a month or so. Oh, I'll need to get a schedule up and the instructors in place." Again, seeming to forget Paige was there, she opened the door to head back inside. "Would you like to see the store, dear?"

Seeing that the lady was overwhelmed, Paige decided to leave her to her mental checklists. "Um, thank you, but I can see you are busy. I'll stop by some other time. Right now, I need to get some food and find a place to stay for the night."

The woman's head snapped over to Paige. "You don't have a place to stay? Are you new to the area?"

"I am. I just drove in from Washington state. I'm moving here and don't have an apartment lined up. Is there a hotel near-by that has reasonable rates?"

"Well, yes, but if you're in need of a place to stay, I have a room right here above the shop you can use. In fact, I was going to rent it out to offset the cost of the suite and employees. It's small, in a shopping center, and connected to a quilt shop; but it's also right next to a grocery store!" The lady smiled, her concern and kindness shining brightly across her face. She had a sweet spirit, and Paige liked her instantly.

"I don't know what to say. This is a surprise and, if I can be honest, it's an answer to prayer if you mean it."

"Oh, I do, and I love hearing that I'm a part of God's handiwork. Here, let me show you the room. There's a separate door to the apartment right next to the shop entrance. Let me go get the keys and you can decide after you see it." The woman disappeared back into her quilt shop and came out faster than Paige had thought possible after seeing her completely overwhelmed a couple of minutes ago. "Here it is. The door has a separate lock so you can be safe and confident. It doesn't have a buzzer or speaker system; you'll need to coordinate leaving this outer door open for folks coming over."

The door was wrought iron and well cared for. It was another sign that this property was loved a great deal by someone. The door led to a staircase that was a little steeper than Paige expected, but easy to manage. The interior was painted in neutrals and led to a small landing where a brown door with a tall, plastic plant with red flowers next to it awaited the two women. Thrilled there was no graffiti or smell, Paige's heart was already galloping with excitement. God had provided way more than she could have ever dreamed.

"This lock has a different key than the first door. Again, it doesn't go to anything else. Only you, the landlord, and I will have one. There's also the ability to lock it from the inside to be sure no one can get in." The shop-keeper opened the door and Paige walked into her second answered prayer: the apartment. The first answer had been the sweet shop-keeper herself.

Want to read more of Paper Treasures? *Head over to Amazon.*

Made in the USA
Middletown, DE
16 March 2021

35229844R00071